DELICIOUS FOOD MISHAPS

FANTASTIC FAILURES
From Flops to Fortune

MARTIN GITLIN

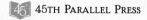

45TH PARALLEL PRESS

Published in the United States of America by Cherry Lake Publishing Group
Ann Arbor, Michigan
www.cherrylakepublishing.com

Reading Adviser: Beth Walker Gambro, MS, Ed., Reading Consultant, Yorkville, IL
Series Adviser: Virginia Loh-Hagan
Book Designer: Frame25 Productions

Photo Credits: © Brendan Lekan/Shutterstock, cover, title page; © Better World Pictures/Shutterstock, 4; © Cast of Thousands/Shutterstock, 5; Unknown author, Public domain, via Wikimedia Commons, 7; © guruXOX/Shutterstock, 8; © Jon Rehg/Shutterstock, 9; Public Domain, Google-digitized, 10; Kimberly Vardeman from Lubbock, TX, USA, CC BY 2.0 via Wikimedia Commons, 11; © tmcphotos/Shutterstock, 12; Unknown source, Public domain, via Wikimedia Commons, 15; Public Domain, Records of District Courts of the United States, RG 21 via National Archives, 16; Public Domain, National Archives, 17; Public Domain, National Archives, 18; GRUBBXDN, Public domain, via Wikimedia Commons, 19; © PasuL/Shutterstock, 20; Unknown author, Public domain, via Wikimedia Commons, 23; Internet Archive Book Images, No restrictions, via Wikimedia Commons, 24; © Wako Megumi/Shutterstock, 25; © Maksim Ladouski/Shutterstock, 26; Laura Scudder potato chip label, Public domain, via Wikimedia Commons, 27; © MDV Edwards/Shutterstock, 28; © Oleg Krugliak/Shutterstock, 29; © Meeko Media/Shutterstock, 32

45th Parallel Press is an imprint of Cherry Lake Publishing Group.

Library of Congress Cataloging-in-Publication Data has been filed and is available at catalog.loc.gov

Cherry Lake Publishing would like to acknowledge the work of the Partnership for 21st Century Learning, a network of Battelle for Kids. Please visit Battelle for Kids online for more information.

Printed in the United States of America

Note from publisher: Websites change regularly, and their future contents are outside of our control. Supervise children when conducting any recommended online searches for extended learning opportunities.

Contents

INTRODUCTION

"If at first you don't succeed, try, try again." This is an old saying. It's been said a lot. And it's a great tip. Failure is part of life. It's not bad. It can have good results. People must not let failure defeat them. They should keep trying. Failing can lead to success.

Food and drink makers learn from their mistakes. They know about failing. They have ideas. They test their ideas. But not all ideas work. Some ideas **flop**. *Flop* means to fail. Ideas may not work as planned.

Successful people don't give up. They solve problems. They find other uses for flops. They turn flops into fortunes.

The food business has many examples. Many great products started as failures. These failures worked out. They became tasty treats. They became very popular.

Successful food and drink makers had open minds. They tested new ideas. They showed **persistence**. Persisting means not quitting. Their hard work paid off. That is a lesson everyone can learn.

CHAPTER 1

Chocolate Chip Cookies: The Yummy Accident

....

Ruth Graves Wakefield loved making sweet treats. She worked at the Toll House Inn. This inn was in Massachusetts. Wakefield ran it with her husband. His name was Kenneth.

Wakefield baked for her guests. She made many meals. She was proud of her tasty foods. She loved making desserts best. She made pies. She made cakes. She baked cookies.

The year was 1930. Wakefield was making a batch of cookies. She used a popular **recipe**. Recipes are cooking instructions. Wakefield wanted to make chocolate butter drop do cookies. She had made them before. This time, there was a problem. Wakefield ran out of Baker's Chocolate. Baker's Chocolate has no added sugar. It's bitter. It's used for baking. It's not meant to be eaten by itself.

Ruth Graves Wakefield (1903-1977)

So Wakefield used what she had. Nestle is a food and drink company. Wakefield used Nestle semi-sweet chocolate. She chopped it up. She added it to her cookies. She expected the same result. She thought the chocolate would melt. She thought it would spread around the cookie. But that didn't happen. The chocolate pieces didn't lose their shape. They just got softer. They cookies were gooey. They were sweet.

Wakefield gave them to her guests. They loved them. The cookies became a hit. Wakefield kept making them. She named them the "Chocolate Crunch Cookie." Wakefield had invented a new cookie. Many think it's the world's most popular cookie recipe.

Wakefield shared her invention. Her recipe appeared in newspapers. It was shared on the radio. It was featured on a baking show. The show was called *The Betty Crocker Cooking School of the Air*. Betty Crocker wasn't a real person. She was a character created by a company. The character promoted food and recipes.

Wakefield became famous. Folks were gobbling down her new cookie. Her recipe became even more popular in 1936. That is when she published a cookbook. Her cookbook was called *Toll House Tried and True Recipes*. It featured her "Chocolate Crunch Cookie" recipe.

Wakefield gave Nestle the recipe in 1939. Nestle renamed them Toll House cookies. The company gave Wakefield free chocolate for life.

These cookies are yummy. They're also easy and cheap to make. They were popular during World War II (1939–1945). They were sent overseas to U.S. soldiers. Soon, they were everywhere. They were sold to restaurants. The frozen dough was sold in supermarkets.

Today, the cookies are known as chocolate chip cookies. They're loved by many. They're popular around the world. They're eaten in different ways. In some countries, they're topped with chocolate sauce. Then they're eaten with a knife and fork.

Chocolate chip cookies are a great treat. Thank goodness for Wakefield's failed recipe. Her mistake was forgetting to buy Baker's Chocolate. What a yummy mistake!

FLOPPED!
New Coke

There are Coca-Cola (or Coke) fans. There are Pepsi fans. People debate which one tastes better. This soda war has been going on for years. Each company tries to outdo the other. In April 1985, the makers of Coke had an idea. They changed Coke's formula. They made it sweeter. They wanted it to taste more like Pepsi. But Coke fans hated the new taste. Coke had lost the war to Pepsi. The Coca-Cola Company admitted its mistake. It brought back the old Coke formula. It kept selling New Coke. In 1990, it changed its name to Coke II. That did not last either. Coke II was gone by 2002. Only the original Coke remained. And that is how its fans want it.

CHAPTER 2

Forgetfulness + a Cold Night = the Popsicle

Frank Epperson lived in San Francisco, California. In 1905, he made history. He was just 11 years old.

It was a cold night. Epperson wanted something sweet. He mixed sugary soda powder with water. Then he forgot about it. He left it outside. The mixture froze. Epperson saw it the next morning. It looked sweet. It looked tasty. He licked it. It was yummy! Epperson was inspired. He gave his invention a name. He called it the Epsicle. He combined his last name and *icicle*.

He knew his friends would like them. He made more. He sold them around his neighborhood. His Epsicle was a hit. He grew his business. He sold the treats at Neptune Beach. Neptune Beach is in California. It's an amusement park. It was very popular. It had roller coasters. It had a big swimming pool. The weather was warm. It was a great place to sell cold treats. Kids loved his Epsicle. They were cheap. They were tasty.

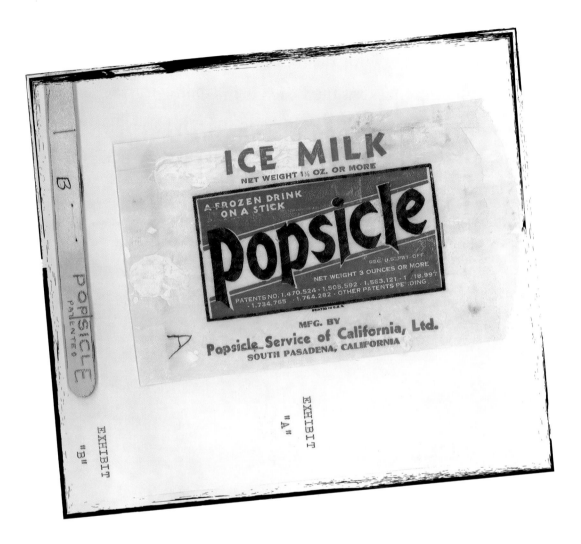

Epperson applied for a **patent**. He did this in 1924. Patents protect inventors' rights. He was the only person who could sell Epsicles. His patent showed how to make the perfect ice pop. It even shared which woods worked best for the stick.

Later, Epperson's kids gave him a tip. They urged him to change the treat's name. They said they should be called "popsicles." After all, Epperson was their "pop." Pop means father. Epperson started the Popsicle Corporation. He worked with a movie company. They sold Popsicles during movies. They sold them at amusement parks. One stand sold 8,000 in one day.

Popsicle Corporation partnered with Joe Lowe. Lowe ran the Joe Lowe Company. Lowe knew how to make money. He sold food across the country. He added a second stick to the popsicle. He sold it for 5 cents.

But Popsicle had a problem. Lots of people were putting frozen treats on sticks. Popsicle **sued** other companies. Sued means took to court. Other companies sued Popsicle. Each company claimed the other was copying their product.

Good Humor was a company that sued Popsicle. Good Humor also sold frozen treats. Good Humor sold ice cream on sticks. Good Humor claimed Lowe was selling the same product. The two companies agreed to a **compromise**. Compromise means to agree. It was decided Popsicle would sell only treats based in water. Good Humor would sell only ice cream.

The Popsicle Corporation grew into a huge company. It was then sold to Unilever. Unilever is another big food company. This happened in 1989. Unilever later bought Good Humor. It could now make whatever frozen treat it wanted.

The Popsicle is still popular today. It never melted away. It's the perfect treat on a hot day. About 2 billion are sold every year. Epperson's forgetfulness and a cold night inspired a beloved treat.

FLOPPED!

Post's Corn-Fetti Flakes

Frosted Flakes is a popular cereal. It hit the market in 1952. But there was a cereal that came before it. It was called Corn-Fetti. Corn-Fetti was made by Post. Post is a cereal company. Corn-Fetti didn't sell well. It was too hard. It was like eating glass. Kellogg's is another cereal company. It liked the idea of a frosted flake. It improved upon Corn-Fetti. It launched Frosted Flakes a year later. The cereal was not as hard. People liked it more than Corn-Fetti. Corn-Fetti stuck around for 8 years. It was gone in 1959. It couldn't compete with Frosted Flakes.

CHAPTER 3

A Customer Complaint Creates Potato Chips

Millions of people eat potato chips every day. But they never think about George Crum. And they should. Most folks have never heard of Crum. But the potato chip might not exist without him.

Crum was a Black and Indigenous American. He was a chef in 1853. He worked at the Moon Lake Lodge Resort. The resort was in Saratoga Springs, New York.

Crum made many dishes using potatoes. One was French fries. Crum cut the potatoes. Then he fried them.

One customer didn't like his fries. He complained. He said they were too thick. He said they were too soft. Crum returned to the kitchen. He listened to the feedback. He tried to improve his fries. He cut the potatoes thinner. He fried them longer. The fries came out crispy.

George Crum and "Aunt Kate" Weeks in 1853

The customer loved his new creation. So did others. The thin, crispy fries were a hit. Many asked for them. They became known as "Saratoga Chips."

There are different stories about the invention of these chips. Some people claim Crum was mad. They say he disliked the customer. So he overcooked the new batch. Others claim his sister invented the chips.

Empire Spring, Saratoga.

His sister's name was Kate. She also worked at the resort. People say she dropped potatoes into hot fat by accident. Another story says Crum and Kate's brother-in-law made the chips. His name was Peter Francis.

Either way, potato chips were invented. Crum opened his own restaurant in 1860. It was called Crum's Place. He mostly served rich people. A basket of Saratoga Chips was placed on every table. Crum's Place closed in 1890. But the chips have lived on. They were sold in grocery stores. They were first sold in Cleveland in 1895.

New **innovations** boosted sales. Innovations are new creations. Chips were first stored in barrels. They were served in paper bags. They got stale fast. Then Laura Scudder had an idea. This happened in 1926. Scudder worked in a family chip business. She created bags lined with wax paper. This kept chips fresher longer. It also stopped them from breaking apart.

Another change came in 1954. It happened in Ireland. Joe "Spud" Murphy owned a potato chip company. He began using different flavors. Examples were cheese and onion. More flavors were invented. Different flavors became popular in different countries. Many Americans prefer barbecue chips. **Paprika** chips are popular in Germany. Paprika is a spice. Some in India like mint flavored chips. Ham flavor is a hit in Spain.

It's a good thing Crum listened to a customer complaint. Feedback and failure are keys to success.

FLOPPED!

Colgate . . . *TV Dinners?*

Colgate is a company. It makes toothpaste. In 1982, it did something shocking. And most think it was dumb. Colgate tried to make dinners. It started a Colgate Kitchen brand. It offered chicken and crab. It was a huge failure. Even its toothpaste sales dropped. Going from toothpaste to meals was too much.

LEARN MORE

Books

America's Test Kitchen. *The Complete Cookbook for Young Scientists: Good Science Makes Great Food: 70+ Recipes, Experiments, & Activities*. Boston: America's Test Kitchen Kids, 2021.

Biberdorf, Kate. *Kate the Chemist: The Awesome Book of Edible Experiments for Kids*. New York: Philomel Books, 2021.

Kenney, Daniel. *I Won't Give Up*. Trendwood Press, 2018.

Loh-Hagan, Virginia. *Food*. Ann Arbor, MI: Cherry Lake Publishing, 2021.

Loh-Hagan, Virginia. *Weird Science: Food*. Ann Arbor, MI: Cherry Lake Publishing, 2022.

Websites

With an adult, explore more online with these suggested searches.

Ezra Jack Keats Foundation

"Snack Shack," Whyville

GLOSSARY

compromise (KAM-pruh-myez) a deal that attempts to be fair to both parties

flop (FLAHP) to fail

innovations (ih-nuh-VAY-shuhnz) new ideas, methods, or products

paprika (puh-PREE-kuh) a mild red pepper powder

patent (PA-tuhnt) government document allowing someone the sole right to make and sell an invention

persistence (per-SIH-stuhns) the will to keep trying after first failing or experiencing challenges

recipe (REH-suh-pee) a set of instructions for making food

sued (SOOD) took another party to court over a dispute

INDEX

ABOUT THE AUTHOR

Martin Gitlin is an educational book author based in Connecticut. He won more than 45 awards as a newspaper sportswriter from 1991 to 2002. Included was a first-place award from the Associated Press for his coverage of the 1995 World Series. He has had more than 200 books published since 2006. Most of them were written for students.